MW01489259

This book belongs to

_____

GOAL PLANNING AND TRACKER JOURNAL
A Journal to Success

By Angela C Williams

This journal is specially designed to help you plan and keep track of your goals for the span of 12 months. Its unique design allows you to record multiple short and long term goals, prioritize them, and select four of them to focus on over the course of a year, as well as track short term monthly goals. Goal setting and planning is the first step to achieving success. This journal will provide you with instructions and examples on how to successfully plan and track goals as well as comprehensive writing space to record your information.

ISBN 978-0-6151-6138-9

Special bulk order discounts may be available. Contact the publisher for details.

For Publisher Information Contact:
Angela C. Williams
claudetteexpressions@yahoo.com

TABLE OF CONTENTS

Instructions for Using Journal

USING THE GOAL SETTING LISTS (2 Sheets)
**This list is designed to allow you to list all of the goals you would like to achieve. You can list all goals, indicate if they are long or short term, indicate your target completion date, and prioritize them. This will help you determine your top 4 goals to start working towards in this journal.

USING THE GOAL PRIORITIZATION GUIDES (4 Sheets) (See sample-Table 1)
**This guide will establish your successful planning. There are 4 Goal Prioritization Guides throughout this book to allow you the opportunity to set and plan multiple goals. Your goals may consist of areas within the following categories; Health and Fitness, Family and Relationship, Time Management and Organizational, Personal Finance, Career, Education and Training, Personal Growth, Leisure and Hobbies or Recreation, and Home Improvement.

Determine the Goal to Achieve
This should be specific as to what you plan to achieve. If you have multiple goals that are similar, track them separately to avoid overlooking potential goal planning needs.

Determine Why You Want to Achieve the Goal
This should also be specific. Determining why you want to achieve it will help you establish a purpose and give your goal more meaning for you. When tracking your goals monthly, periodically review your reason for wanting to achieve it.

Determine Your Specific Plan to Implement Your Goal
This is your specific plan to help you achieve your goal. Establish your priorities. What will you begin to do differently to achieve it? What information do you need to get started? Who will you tell to help hold you accountable? Etc.

Determine Area(s) of Specific Focus
What within your goal is your target? Specify your focus area within your goal.

Determine the Target Completion Date
Establishing a target completion date is an important part of working towards your goal. But remember, target dates can be adjusted if necessary. The most important thing is to have a target date to strive towards.

Establish the Priority
How important is this goal to you? This will help you prioritize and balance all of your goals.

Instructions for Using Journal...continued

USING THE MONTHLY PROGRESS TRACKER (9 Sheets) (See sample-Table 2)

**After you have completed the Goal Prioritization Guide, you may begin using the Monthly Progress Tracker to record your progress. For each of the 4 Goal Prioritization Guides, there are 9 pages consisting of room to record monthly results to track monthly progress and setbacks.

Progress/Accomplishments
Indicate in this column your current month's accomplishments and progress towards your goals

Setbacks
Indicate in this column any setbacks to your goals. These could be in or out of your control. This will give you the ability to review reasons for stifled progress

What I Will Do Differently
Indicate in this column what you will do differently going forward, if anything based on your accomplishments and setbacks.

SUGGESTIONS FOR SUCCESS WITH THIS JOURNAL

Establish a Partner
Establishing a partner can help you become more accountable to achieve your goals. Set up monthly meetings to meet and discuss each others progress and setbacks. Discuss what you should do going forward. Openly discussing your goal planning will help keep it fresh in your mind and helps you to become more focused.

Periodically Review your Goal Prioritization Guide details
Reviewing your purpose information periodically will help to keep the reasons for your goals fresh. Update your reason for desiring to achieve a goal as necessary. Also, use the space provided for your 4 goals in the Table of Contents for easy reference.

Use One Goal Prioritization Guide and Monthly Progress Tracking Per Goal
Be sure to use one Goal Prioritization Guide and Monthly Progress Tracking per goal to ensure you are able to adequately track success for your goals. This journal is designed to track 4 goals throughout a 12 month period.

Be Committed
Commit yourself to tracking your progress. Review and track your progress a minimum of monthly. Always remember, there is a difference between those who can and those who will.

Use the Convenient Bonus Tracking Sheets at Back of Journal
This journal also includes 4 Diet Tracking sheets, 4 Weight and Blood Pressure Tracking sheets, and 12 Monthly Budget and Short Term Monthly Goal Tracker Sheets at the end of this book for your convenience. You may use them to help you track these items if your goal fits into one or more of these categories. The Diet Tracking sheet will give you 48 days to view your eating habits. The Weight/Blood Pressure Sheets will give you a sufficient source for tracking those numbers as well. The Short Term Goal tracker sheets allow you to focus monthly on goals you have not selected as one of your major 4 goals.

Table 1-Samples—Goal Prioritization Guide

Goal to Achieve	Why do you want to achieve this goal?	What is your plan to implement?	Area of Focus?	Target Completion Date	Your Priority Scale 1=high 2=medium 3=low
Payoff credit card bill	Free up money, reduce interest debt, live within means, use cards only when necessary and payoff within month of purchase	Go to web-site to determine amount needed to pay monthly to pay off bills by May 2012-Stash away credit cards and live within current cash means.	Capital One Card	5/1/2012	1
Lose Weight	Fit into clothes, feel better about self, live healthier due to health issues associated with weight	Determine appropriate weight for height, and healthy waist measurement (less than 35" for women and 40" for men). Achieve and maintain relative weight and waist.	Waist=33; Weight=145	12/1/2007	2
Exercise	Feel better; live healthier	Exercise a minimum of 3 times a week	Abdomen/Waist; Video tapes; Walking; Bicycling	Ongoing	1
Eat healthier	Feel better; live healthier	Track food intake; Eat more healthy foods than fast food	Reduce fast food	Ongoing	1
Eliminate House Clutter	Make room for necessities; Feel better: Make my home a clean haven; Organize better	Throw away old items, give away items not used/needed (give to goodwill; have a yard sale)	Guest room closet; bedroom closet; attic	9/1/2007	2
Fit in Hobby time	Do something I enjoy to help lift my spirit	Set aside 2 hours each week to focus on hobby	Writing	Ongoing	2

Table 2-Samples—Monthly Progress Tracker

Date	Progress/Accomplishments	Setbacks	What I will do differently
7-5-07	Cutup credit card	Opened up store credit card to get sale item	Will pay off store credit card, cut it up and go back to original plan to live within means.
7-28-07	Spent 2 hours today writing	Did not write 2 hours each week this month	Will reorganize time to ensure 2 hours are spent each week on writing.

"The goals you set to conquer will determine your future"

GOAL SETTING LIST

Goals to Achieve	Indicate Long or Short Term	Target Completion Date	Your Priority Scale 1=high 2=medium 3=low
A - #3,000 for 4 weeks 1 ☆	Short	MAY 1, 17'	1
A - Become MANAGER —	Short	June 1	1
A - 5K in CASH (not including BANK)	Short	July 1	2
D - 10 Person OFFICE	Short	MAY 1	2
D - Debt PAID OFF	Short	June 1	1
D - Get in SHAPE	Short	June 1	2

"Value your time now and in the future; follow through"

GOAL SETTING LIST

Goals to Achieve	Indicate Long or Short Term	Target Completion Date	Your Priority Scale 1=high 2=medium 3=low

"Life is worth it! Go ahead and live it!"

GOAL PRIORITIZATION GUIDE-ONE	
Goal to Achieve	
Why do you want to achieve this goal?	
What is your plan to implement?	
Area of Focus?	
Target Completion Date	
Your Priority Scale *1=high 2=medium* *3=low*	

Monthly Progress Tracker-Goal One

Current Month/Date:

Progress/Accomplishments	
Setbacks	
What I will do differently	

Monthly Progress Tracker-Goal One

Current Month/Date:

Progress/Accomplishments	
Setbacks	
What I will do differently	

Monthly Progress Tracker-Goal One

Current Month/Date:

Progress/Accomplishments	
Setbacks	
What I will do differently	

Monthly Progress Tracker-Goal One

Current Month/Date:

Progress/Accomplishments	
Setbacks	
What I will do differently	

Monthly Progress Tracker-Goal One

Current Month/Date:	
Progress/Accomplishments	
Setbacks	
What I will do differently	

Monthly Progress Tracker-Goal One

Current Month/Date:	
Progress/Accomplishments	
Setbacks	
What I will do differently	

Monthly Progress Tracker-Goal One

Current Month/Date:

Progress/Accomplishments	
Setbacks	
What I will do differently	

Monthly Progress Tracker-Goal One

Current Month/Date:

Progress/Accomplishments	
Setbacks	
What I will do differently	

Monthly Progress Tracker-Goal One

Current Month/Date:

Progress/Accomplishments	
Setbacks	
What I will do differently	

Monthly Progress Tracker-Goal One

Current Month/Date:

Progress/Accomplishments	
Setbacks	
What I will do differently	

Monthly Progress Tracker-Goal One

Current Month/Date:	
Progress/Accomplishments	
Setbacks	
What I will do differently	

Monthly Progress Tracker-Goal One

Current Month/Date:	
Progress/Accomplishments	
Setbacks	
What I will do differently	

Monthly Progress Tracker-Goal One

Current Month/Date:

Progress/Accomplishments	
Setbacks	
What I will do differently	

Monthly Progress Tracker-Goal One

Current Month/Date:

Progress/Accomplishments	
Setbacks	
What I will do differently	

Monthly Progress Tracker-Goal One

Current Month/Date:

Progress/Accomplishments	
Setbacks	
What I will do differently	

Monthly Progress Tracker-Goal One

Current Month/Date:

Progress/Accomplishments	
Setbacks	
What I will do differently	

Monthly Progress Tracker-Goal One

Current Month/Date:

Progress/Accomplishments	
Setbacks	
What I will do differently	

Monthly Progress Tracker-Goal One

Current Month/Date:

Progress/Accomplishments	
Setbacks	
What I will do differently	

"You are your own worst and best critic. Criticize wisely."

GOAL PRIORITIZATION GUIDE-TWO

Goal to Achieve	
Why do you want to achieve this goal?	
What is your plan to implement?	
Area of Focus?	
Target Completion Date	
Your Priority Scale *1=high 2=medium* *3=low*	

Monthly Progress Tracker-Goal Two

Current Month/Date:

Progress/Accomplishments	
Setbacks	
What I will do differently	

Monthly Progress Tracker-Goal Two

Current Month/Date:

Progress/Accomplishments	
Setbacks	
What I will do differently	

Monthly Progress Tracker-Goal Two

Current Month/Date:

Progress/Accomplishments	
Setbacks	
What I will do differently	

Monthly Progress Tracker-Goal Two

Current Month/Date:

Progress/Accomplishments	
Setbacks	
What I will do differently	

Monthly Progress Tracker-Goal Two

Current Month/Date:

Progress/Accomplishments	
Setbacks	
What I will do differently	

Monthly Progress Tracker-Goal Two

Current Month/Date:

Progress/Accomplishments	
Setbacks	
What I will do differently	

Monthly Progress Tracker-Goal Two

Current Month/Date:

Progress/Accomplishments	
Setbacks	
What I will do differently	

Monthly Progress Tracker-Goal Two

Current Month/Date:

Progress/Accomplishments	
Setbacks	
What I will do differently	

Monthly Progress Tracker-Goal Two

Current Month/Date:

Progress/Accomplishments	
Setbacks	
What I will do differently	

Monthly Progress Tracker-Goal Two

Current Month/Date:

Progress/Accomplishments	
Setbacks	
What I will do differently	

Monthly Progress Tracker-Goal Two

Current Month/Date:

Progress/Accomplishments	
Setbacks	
What I will do differently	

Monthly Progress Tracker-Goal Two

Current Month/Date:

Progress/Accomplishments	
Setbacks	
What I will do differently	

Monthly Progress Tracker-Goal Two

Current Month/Date:

Progress/Accomplishments	
Setbacks	
What I will do differently	

Monthly Progress Tracker-Goal Two

Current Month/Date:

Progress/Accomplishments	
Setbacks	
What I will do differently	

Monthly Progress Tracker-Goal Two

Current Month/Date:

Progress/Accomplishments	
Setbacks	
What I will do differently	

Monthly Progress Tracker-Goal Two

Current Month/Date:

Progress/Accomplishments	
Setbacks	
What I will do differently	

Monthly Progress Tracker-Goal Two

Current Month/Date:

Progress/Accomplishments	
Setbacks	
What I will do differently	

Monthly Progress Tracker-Goal Two

Current Month/Date:

Progress/Accomplishments	
Setbacks	
What I will do differently	

"Take advantage of your opportunities. There is so much more life has to offer."

GOAL PRIORITIZATION GUIDE-THREE	
Goal to Achieve	
Why do you want to achieve this goal?	
What is your plan to implement?	
Area of Focus?	
Target Completion Date	
Your Priority Scale *1=high 2=medium 3=low*	

Monthly Progress Tracker-Goal Three

Current Month/Date:

Progress/Accomplishments	
Setbacks	
What I will do differently	

Monthly Progress Tracker-Goal Three

Current Month/Date:

Progress/Accomplishments	
Setbacks	
What I will do differently	

Monthly Progress Tracker-Goal Three

Current Month/Date:

Progress/Accomplishments	
Setbacks	
What I will do differently	

Monthly Progress Tracker-Goal Three

Current Month/Date:

Progress/Accomplishments	
Setbacks	
What I will do differently	

Monthly Progress Tracker-Goal Three

Current Month/Date:

Progress/Accomplishments	
Setbacks	
What I will do differently	

Monthly Progress Tracker-Goal Three

Current Month/Date:

Progress/Accomplishments	
Setbacks	
What I will do differently	

Monthly Progress Tracker-Goal Three

Current Month/Date:

Progress/Accomplishments	
Setbacks	
What I will do differently	

Monthly Progress Tracker-Goal Three

Current Month/Date:

Progress/Accomplishments	
Setbacks	
What I will do differently	

Monthly Progress Tracker-Goal Three

Current Month/Date:

Progress/Accomplishments	
Setbacks	
What I will do differently	

Monthly Progress Tracker-Goal Three

Current Month/Date:

Progress/Accomplishments	
Setbacks	
What I will do differently	

Monthly Progress Tracker-Goal Three

Current Month/Date:

Progress/Accomplishments	
Setbacks	
What I will do differently	

Monthly Progress Tracker-Goal Three

Current Month/Date:

Progress/Accomplishments	
Setbacks	
What I will do differently	

Monthly Progress Tracker-Goal Three

Current Month/Date:

Progress/Accomplishments	
Setbacks	
What I will do differently	

Monthly Progress Tracker-Goal Three

Current Month/Date:

Progress/Accomplishments	
Setbacks	
What I will do differently	

Monthly Progress Tracker-Goal Three

Current Month/Date:

Progress/Accomplishments	
Setbacks	
What I will do differently	

Monthly Progress Tracker-Goal Three

Current Month/Date:

Progress/Accomplishments	
Setbacks	
What I will do differently	

Monthly Progress Tracker-Goal Three

Current Month/Date:

Progress/Accomplishments	
Setbacks	
What I will do differently	

Monthly Progress Tracker-Goal Three

Current Month/Date:

Progress/Accomplishments	
Setbacks	
What I will do differently	

"Keep moving forward. It's hard to see moving backwards."

GOAL PRIORITIZATION GUIDE-FOUR	
Goal to Achieve	
Why do you want to achieve this goal?	
What is your plan to implement?	
Area of Focus?	
Target Completion Date	
Your Priority Scale *1=high 2=medium* *3=low*	

Monthly Progress Tracker-Goal Four

Current Month/Date:	
Progress/Accomplishments	
Setbacks	
What I will do differently	

Monthly Progress Tracker-Goal Four

Current Month/Date:	
Progress/Accomplishments	
Setbacks	
What I will do differently	

Monthly Progress Tracker-Goal Four

Current Month/Date:

Progress/Accomplishments	
Setbacks	
What I will do differently	

Monthly Progress Tracker-Goal Four

Current Month/Date:

Progress/Accomplishments	
Setbacks	
What I will do differently	

Monthly Progress Tracker-Goal Four

Current Month/Date:	
Progress/Accomplishments	
Setbacks	
What I will do differently	

Monthly Progress Tracker-Goal Four

Current Month/Date:	
Progress/Accomplishments	
Setbacks	
What I will do differently	

Monthly Progress Tracker-Goal Four

Current Month/Date:

Progress/Accomplishments	
Setbacks	
What I will do differently	

Monthly Progress Tracker-Goal Four

Current Month/Date:

Progress/Accomplishments	
Setbacks	
What I will do differently	

Monthly Progress Tracker-Goal Four

Current Month/Date:

Progress/Accomplishments	
Setbacks	
What I will do differently	

Monthly Progress Tracker-Goal Four

Current Month/Date:

Progress/Accomplishments	
Setbacks	
What I will do differently	

Monthly Progress Tracker-Goal Four

Current Month/Date:

Progress/Accomplishments	
Setbacks	
What I will do differently	

Monthly Progress Tracker-Goal Four

Current Month/Date:

Progress/Accomplishments	
Setbacks	
What I will do differently	

Monthly Progress Tracker-Goal Four

Current Month/Date:

Progress/Accomplishments	
Setbacks	
What I will do differently	

Monthly Progress Tracker-Goal Four

Current Month/Date:

Progress/Accomplishments	
Setbacks	
What I will do differently	

Monthly Progress Tracker-Goal Four

Current Month/Date:

Progress/Accomplishments	
Setbacks	
What I will do differently	

Monthly Progress Tracker-Goal Four

Current Month/Date:

Progress/Accomplishments	
Setbacks	
What I will do differently	

Monthly Progress Tracker-Goal Four

Current Month/Date:

Progress/Accomplishments	
Setbacks	
What I will do differently	

Monthly Progress Tracker-Goal Four

Current Month/Date:

Progress/Accomplishments	
Setbacks	
What I will do differently	

DIET TRACKING					
Breakfast		**Lunch**	**Dinner**	**Snack**
Date	Items	Items	Items	Items

DIET TRACKING

Breakfast		Lunch	Dinner	Snack
Date	Items	Items	Items	Items

DIET TRACKING

Breakfast		Lunch	Dinner	Snack
Date	Items	Items	Items	Items

DIET TRACKING

	Breakfast	Lunch	Dinner	Snack
Date	Items	Items	Items	Items

DIET TRACKING

	Breakfast	Lunch	Dinner	Snack
Date	Items	Items	Items	Items

DIET TRACKING

Breakfast		Lunch	Dinner	Snack
Date	Items	Items	Items	Items

WEIGHT/BLOOD PRESSURE TRACKING

Date	Time	BP	Weight	Date	Time	BP	Weight

WEIGHT/BLOOD PRESSURE TRACKING

Date	Time	BP	Weight	Date	Time	BP	Weight

WEIGHT/BLOOD PRESSURE TRACKING

Date	Time	BP	Weight	Date	Time	BP	Weight

WEIGHT/BLOOD PRESSURE TRACKING

Date	Time	BP	Weight	Date	Time	BP	Weight

Monthly Budget Tracking

Expenses	Amount Due	Due Date	Auto Pay (Y or N)	Pay Method Check=CK Debit=DB Credit=CR	Amt Paid	Date Paid
Total Expenses						
Monthly Income						
Disposable Income (Monthly Income minus total Expenses; Negative amount equals insufficient funds)						

Monthly Budget Tracking

Expenses	Amount Due	Due Date	Auto Pay (Y or N)	Pay Method Check=CK Debit=DB Credit=CR	Amt Paid	Date Paid
Total Expenses						
Monthly Income						
Disposable Income (Monthly Income minus total Expenses; Negative amount equals insufficient funds)						

Monthly Budget Tracking

Expenses	Amount Due	Due Date	Auto Pay (Y or N)	Pay Method Check=CK Debit=DB Credit=CR	Amt Paid	Date Paid
Total Expenses						
Monthly Income						
Disposable Income (Monthly Income minus total Expenses; Negative amount equals insufficient funds)						

Monthly Budget Tracking

Expenses	Amount Due	Due Date	Auto Pay (Y or N)	Pay Method Check=CK Debit=DB Credit=CR	Amt Paid	Date Paid
Total Expenses						
Monthly Income						
Disposable Income (Monthly Income minus total Expenses; Negative amount equals insufficient funds)						

Monthly Budget Tracking

Expenses	Amount Due	Due Date	Auto Pay (Y or N)	Pay Method Check=CK Debit=DB Credit=CR	Amt Paid	Date Paid
Total Expenses						
Monthly Income						
Disposable Income (Monthly Income minus total Expenses; Negative amount equals insufficient funds)						

Monthly Budget Tracking

Expenses	Amount Due	Due Date	Auto Pay (Y or N)	Pay Method Check=CK Debit=DB Credit=CR	Amt Paid	Date Paid
Total Expenses						
Monthly Income						
Disposable Income (Monthly Income minus total Expenses; Negative amount equals insufficient funds)						

Monthly Budget Tracking

Expenses	Amount Due	Due Date	Auto Pay (Y or N)	Pay Method Check=CK Debit=DB Credit=CR	Amt Paid	Date Paid
Total Expenses						
Monthly Income						
Disposable Income (Monthly Income minus total Expenses; Negative amount equals insufficient funds)						

Monthly Budget Tracking

Expenses	Amount Due	Due Date	Auto Pay (Y or N)	Pay Method Check=CK Debit=DB Credit=CR	Amt Paid	Date Paid
Total Expenses						
Monthly Income						
Disposable Income *(Monthly Income minus total Expenses; Negative amount equals insufficient funds)*						

Monthly Budget Tracking

Expenses	Amount Due	Due Date	Auto Pay (Y or N)	Pay Method Check=CK Debit=DB Credit=CR	Amt Paid	Date Paid
Total Expenses						
Monthly Income						
Disposable Income (Monthly Income minus total Expenses; Negative amount equals insufficient funds)						

Monthly Budget Tracking

Expenses	Amount Due	Due Date	Auto Pay (Y or N)	Pay Method Check=CK Debit=DB Credit=CR	Amt Paid	Date Paid
Total Expenses						
Monthly Income						
Disposable Income (Monthly Income minus total Expenses; Negative amount equals insufficient funds)						

Monthly Budget Tracking

Expenses	Amount Due	Due Date	Auto Pay (*Y or N*)	Pay Method *Check=CK* *Debit=DB* *Credit=CR*	Amt Paid	Date Paid
Total Expenses						
Monthly Income						
Disposable Income *(Monthly Income minus total Expenses; Negative amount equals insufficient funds)*						

Monthly Budget Tracking

Expenses	Amount Due	Due Date	Auto Pay (Y or N)	Pay Method Check=CK Debit=DB Credit=CR	Amt Paid	Date Paid
Total Expenses						
Monthly Income						
Disposable Income (Monthly Income minus total Expenses; Negative amount equals insufficient funds)						

"Last month's labors are this month's fruit. Are you enjoying your fruit?"

Short Term Monthly Tracker

Current Month:	
Short Term Goal	
Current Month Accomplishments	
Current Month Setbacks	
Target Completion Date	
Status Complete/Pending/Monthly-Recurring	

Short Term Monthly Tracker

Current Month:	
Short Term Goal	
Current Month Accomplishments	
Current Month Setbacks	
Target Completion Date	
Status Complete/Pending/Monthly-Recurring	

"Make a difference now by setting your goal. You'll enjoy the benefits sooner than later"

Short Term Monthly Tracker

Current Month:

Short Term Goal	
Current Month Accomplishments	
Current Month Setbacks	
Target Completion Date	
Status Complete/Pending/Monthly-Recurring	

Short Term Monthly Tracker

Current Month:

Short Term Goal	
Current Month Accomplishments	
Current Month Setbacks	
Target Completion Date	
Status Complete/Pending/Monthly-Recurring	

"It's not enough to think about it; you must do it."

Short Term Monthly Tracker

Current Month:

Short Term Goal	
Current Month Accomplishments	
Current Month Setbacks	
Target Completion Date	
Status Complete/Pending/Monthly-Recurring	

Short Term Monthly Tracker

Current Month:

Short Term Goal	
Current Month Accomplishments	
Current Month Setbacks	
Target Completion Date	
Status Complete/Pending/Monthly-Recurring	

"Many people can; only a few will. Will you? Track it."

Short Term Monthly Tracker	
Current Month:	
Short Term Goal	
Current Month Accomplishments	
Current Month Setbacks	
Target Completion Date	
Status Complete/Pending/Monthly-Recurring	

Short Term Monthly Tracker	
Current Month:	
Short Term Goal	
Current Month Accomplishments	
Current Month Setbacks	
Target Completion Date	
Status Complete/Pending/Monthly-Recurring	

"If you can visualize it, you can accomplish it."

Short Term Monthly Tracker

Current Month:

Short Term Goal	
Current Month Accomplishments	
Current Month Setbacks	
Target Completion Date	
Status Complete/Pending/Monthly-Recurring	

Short Term Monthly Tracker

Current Month:

Short Term Goal	
Current Month Accomplishments	
Current Month Setbacks	
Target Completion Date	
Status Complete/Pending/Monthly-Recurring	

"Success is for those who want it enough to act."

Short Term Monthly Tracker

Current Month:

Short Term Goal	
Current Month Accomplishments	
Current Month Setbacks	
Target Completion Date	
Status Complete/Pending/Monthly-Recurring	

Short Term Monthly Tracker

Current Month:

Short Term Goal	
Current Month Accomplishments	
Current Month Setbacks	
Target Completion Date	
Status Complete/Pending/Monthly-Recurring	

"It's your life. Take charge of it."

Short Term Monthly Tracker

Current Month:	
Short Term Goal	
Current Month Accomplishments	
Current Month Setbacks	
Target Completion Date	
Status Complete/Pending/Monthly-Recurring	

Short Term Monthly Tracker

Current Month:	
Short Term Goal	
Current Month Accomplishments	
Current Month Setbacks	
Target Completion Date	
Status Complete/Pending/Monthly-Recurring	

"Changes make life and learning more interesting. Organize your need for change."

Short Term Monthly Tracker

Current Month:

Short Term Goal	
Current Month Accomplishments	
Current Month Setbacks	
Target Completion Date	
Status Complete/Pending/Monthly-Recurring	

Short Term Monthly Tracker

Current Month:

Short Term Goal	
Current Month Accomplishments	
Current Month Setbacks	
Target Completion Date	
Status Complete/Pending/Monthly-Recurring	

"Write it, share it, and conquer it. It's your success."

Short Term Monthly Tracker

Current Month:	
Short Term Goal	
Current Month Accomplishments	
Current Month Setbacks	
Target Completion Date	
Status Complete/Pending/Monthly-Recurring	

Short Term Monthly Tracker

Current Month:	
Short Term Goal	
Current Month Accomplishments	
Current Month Setbacks	
Target Completion Date	
Status Complete/Pending/Monthly-Recurring	

"If we can fly the skies, you can make it happen."

Short Term Monthly Tracker

Current Month:

Short Term Goal	
Current Month Accomplishments	
Current Month Setbacks	
Target Completion Date	
Status Complete/Pending/Monthly-Recurring	

Short Term Monthly Tracker

Current Month:

Short Term Goal	
Current Month Accomplishments	
Current Month Setbacks	
Target Completion Date	
Status Complete/Pending/Monthly-Recurring	

"Prioritize your month and achieve your dreams."

Short Term Monthly Tracker

Current Month:	
Short Term Goal	
Current Month Accomplishments	
Current Month Setbacks	
Target Completion Date	
Status Complete/Pending/Monthly-Recurring	

Short Term Monthly Tracker

Current Month:	
Short Term Goal	
Current Month Accomplishments	
Current Month Setbacks	
Target Completion Date	
Status Complete/Pending/Monthly-Recurring	

"One day at a time is all it takes."

Short Term Monthly Tracker

Current Month:

Short Term Goal	
Current Month Accomplishments	
Current Month Setbacks	
Target Completion Date	
Status Complete/Pending/Monthly-Recurring	

Short Term Monthly Tracker

Current Month:

Short Term Goal	
Current Month Accomplishments	
Current Month Setbacks	
Target Completion Date	
Status Complete/Pending/Monthly-Recurring	

CPSIA information can be obtained
at www.ICGtesting.com
Printed in the USA
BVOW04s0719080117

472908BV00004B/237/P